My dad is an astrophysicist.
He studies the universe and all of the life forms that live in it. Planets, stars, comets, asteroids, galaxies, meteors, you name them, he knows all about them.
He helps the scientists at the local space center to discover new life forms in the universe.
He helps the teachers in the schools write lessons for them to teach their students.
I even invited my dad to my elementary school on career day as a guest speaker. My friends were so amazed by what my dad does! Some of them even said they also want a job as an astrophysicist.
That's why my dad is awesome!
He can explain the universe very clearly and in many different ways to many different people.

I learn so much about science and outer space from my dad.

I may not be as smart as he is right now, but someday, I will learn enough about the wonders of our universe to become an astrophysicist just like him. There are many facts that I have already memorized, and I can't wait to study even more! Let's see, I know that the galaxy that we live in is called The Milky Way.

I know that the Solar System is only a small part of what is included in the Milky Way. I know that the sun is at the center of our Solar System. And I also know that there are eight planets in our Solar System that orbit or circle the sun. Some of these planets are very close to the sun, while other planets are very far away. One of the eight planets in our Solar System is the planet that we live on, planet Earth. Earth is the third closest planet to the sun.

I can name all eight planets in our Solar System. Let's see, first there's Mercury, which is the closest planet to the sun.

Mercury is the smallest planet in the Solar System. Then there is Venus which is the second closest planet to the sun.

Venus is made up of clouds that contain sulfuric acid, which is why it has a pale—yellow appearance.

Because Mercury and Venus are the planets that are the closest to the sun, they are very, very hot! Ouch!

Then there's the planet we live on called Earth. Earth is the only planet that is habitable, which means that humans like us and other animal species as small as mice and as large as elephants can live on it. If you are familiar with the story of Goldilocks and the Three Bears, think of Earth as being not too hot, not too cold, but just right. Like Baby Bear's food, chair, and bed.

Getting back to the planets in the Solar System, after planet Earth comes Mars, the red planet.

Mars is composed of mainly soil, sand, and rocks. Mars is like a big dry desert. It looks red because the iron in its soil eventually turns to rust. This rust is like the rust you see on metal objects such as hammers and nails. Red or brown in color with a dull, non—shiny surface.

Next comes Jupiter, the biggest planet of them all. Jupiter has what looks like a red eye on it. This is what is known as The Great Red Spot. Next is the planet Saturn with those bright and colorful rings around it. These rings are made of water and ice. Because water and ice shine when they reflect on the sun, the rings of Saturn look like they are glowing. This is why Saturn appears to be such a colorful planet.

If you look up in the sky at night, sometimes you can see Mercury, Venus, Mars, Jupiter, and Saturn shining oh so brightly.

Rounding out the Solar System are Uranus and Neptune, the farthest planets from the sun. Uranus is known as being the "Sideways Planet." This means that Uranus rotates on its side. Its North Pole and South Pole are like our Equator. Neptune is the eighth and final planet in our Solar System. It is almost as large as Uranus, but not nearly as large as Saturn and Jupiter. Uranus and Neptune both have a blue appearance because of the methane in their atmospheres that absorbs the sun's red light and reflects the sun's blue light back into space. They are very, very cold planets! Brr!

Not only are the planets a major part of our Solar System, but their moons are important too. Most of the planets have at least one moon orbiting around them. Some of the planets do not even have a moon. Mercury and Venus, for example, do not have any moons.

Earth, the planet that we live on, has only one moon. We can sometimes see the moon shining brightly in our sky at night. Earth's moon appears to be about the same size as the sun from where we can see it in the sky. But we know that our moon is much smaller than the sun. The sun just happens to be farther away, making it appear similar to our moon in size.

Mars has two moons. The smallest moons in the entire Solar System orbit Mars. They are named Phobos and Deimos. Both of Mars's moons have a rocky appearance and are not as round in shape as most other moons.

Did you know that Jupiter has ninety-five moons and Saturn has one-hundred and forty-six moons? That's a lot of moons! These moons come in so many different sizes and colors. The largest moon in the entire Solar System is called Ganymede, and it orbits Jupiter. There are other moons that are just as big and are unique in composition and appearance. The second largest moon is called Titan, and it orbits Saturn. Titan is said to be a lot like Earth because it contains rivers, lakes, seas, and yellow clouds. That's why it appears to be solid yellow in color.

Uranus and Neptune also have moons! While they do not have as many moons as Jupiter and Saturn, they have significantly more moons in their orbits than Earth and Mars. Uranus has twenty-eight moons. Of those moons, five are known as the major moons that orbit Uranus. These moons are known by the names Titania, Oberon, Miranda, Ariel, and Umbriel. Neptune has sixteen moons. Of the moons orbiting Neptune, only one is very large and significant, that being Triton.

Did you know that Pluto used to be considered a planet? That's right, on March 24th, 1930, Pluto was officially named the ninth planet in the Solar System after Neptune. Seventy—six years later, it was discovered that Pluto was not large enough in size to be classified as a planet, but rather, Pluto was classified as a dwarf planet. Dwarf planets are often smaller than the largest moons in the Solar System. But dwarf planets also orbit the sun, rather than another planet, meaning they cannot be classified as a moon. Pluto is known to be slightly smaller than planet Earth's own moon. This means that, while Pluto can no longer be labeled as one of the major planets in the Solar System, it still functions like a planet.

Think of the name "dwarf planet" as being a minor planet. A good comparison is how in baseball there are major league teams and minor league teams. Think of dwarf planets in the same way as you would a minor league baseball team. Dwarf planets serve the same purpose as the eight major planets but are not as strong and recognizable as those eight major planets.

We will learn even more about Earth's moon when I tell you about the one activity in outer space that interests my dad the most. Ready for it?

Well, what really fascinates my dad, more than anything, is the occurrence of a total solar eclipse! This happens when the moon is circling around our planet Earth and passes directly in front of the path of the sun, blocking any light from shining down on Earth. When a total solar eclipse is in effect, the sky turns completely black for several minutes. Just like when you are sitting inside of your hallway closet with the lights turned off.

Solar eclipses, some being partial eclipses and others being total eclipses, occur several times a year. However, not everyone on our planet Earth can see a solar eclipse all the time. Sometimes you can watch a solar eclipse if you live in China. Other times, you can watch a solar eclipse if you live in France. And other times, you can watch a solar eclipse if you live in Antarctica. But I don't think a lot of people live in Antarctica. The penguins may be happy to watch a solar eclipse. But anyway, it all depends on what side of Earth is facing the sun when the moon passes in front of it for a few moments. Those are the lucky humans that get to watch a solar eclipse.

I live in the United States and have never watched a total solar eclipse. This will change on April 8th of 2024. That is the day me, my family, and my friends will get to see a total solar eclipse right from the comfort of our own backyard.

Because my dad is an astrophysicist, he knows a lot about solar eclipses. As I mentioned before, I learned from my dad that our Earth's moon may appear to be about the same size as the sun when we look up in the sky at night. However, the moon is closer to Earth than the sun. So, while it seems like the sun and moon are the same size, that is totally not the case. We know from looking at maps and diagrams of our Solar System that our moon is much smaller in size than the sun. If the sun was the same distance away from our Earth as the moon is, we would notice how large the sun actually appears. But would we really? If the sun was that close to the Earth, it would burn every living creature to death, causing the entire planet to become extinct.

What does this have to do with solar eclipses? Well, the size of the moon in relation to the size of the sun is almost the same when viewed from Earth. So, when the moon orbits around the Earth and falls directly in the path of the sun during the day, the daylight is turned off until the moon is out of the sun's way. Then, when the moon passes away from the sun, voila! It's sunny again!

Did you know there are five distinct stages of a total solar eclipse? My dad explained this to me as we anticipate the upcoming eclipse. The first stage is known as First Contact. This is when the moon is just beginning to pass in front of the sun. If you have ever seen what a crescent moon looks like, this is exactly the shape that the sun takes. A crescent sun! First Contact is when the skies begin to darken as the moon makes its way in front of the sun. If you look at the ground, you will notice an effect that creates wavy looking lines of light. These are known as shadow bands. They often resemble "mini" crescent moons.

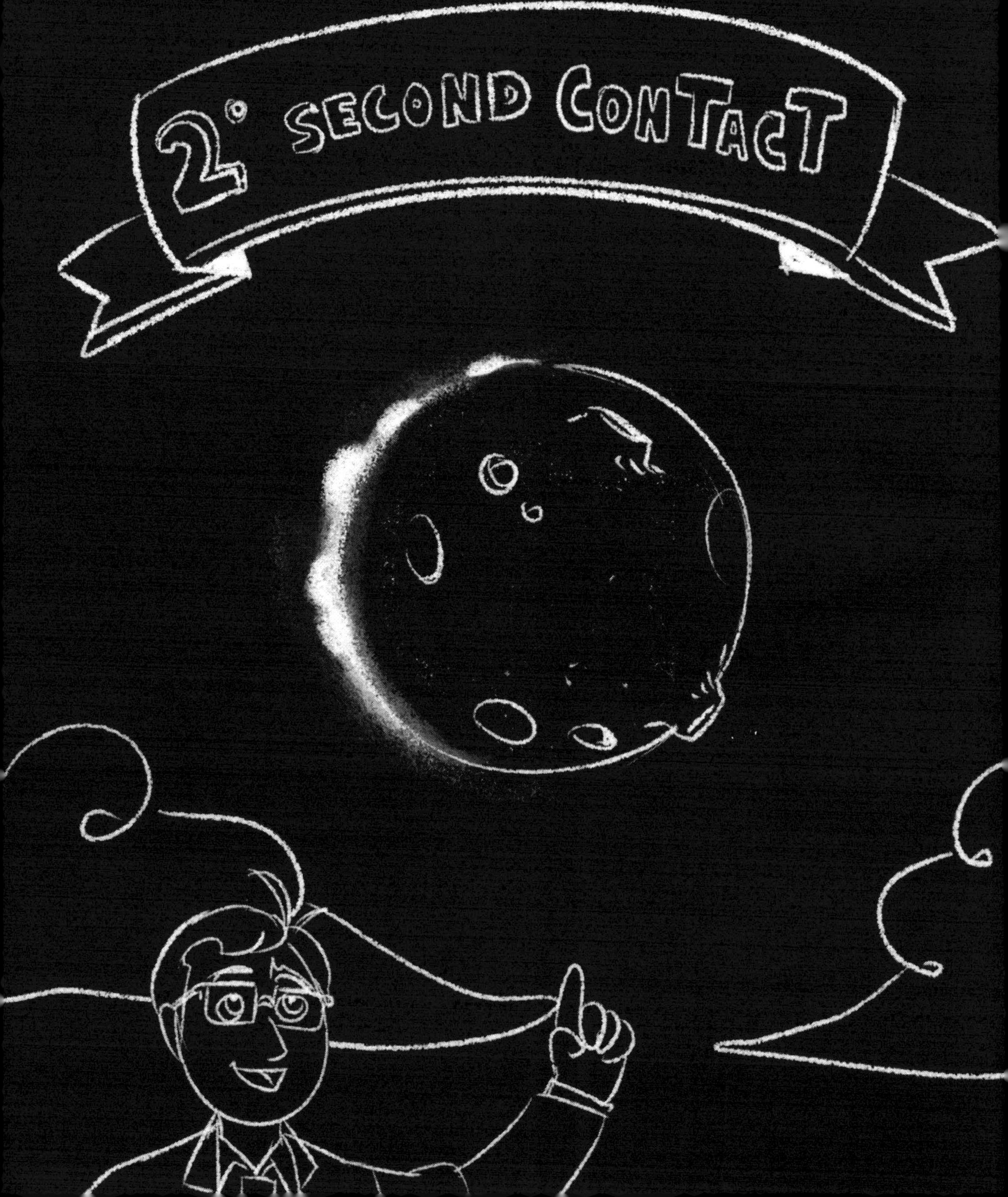
2° SECOND CONTACT

The second state is called Second Contact. It occurs just before the sky goes completely dark. Nearing the end of Second Contact, balls of light appear to outline the glow of the sun surrounding the blackened moon. This is known as Baily's beads. The reason why they look like beads is because the moon's craters help to form the sunlight into the shape of beads. As the eclipse continues, the beads disappear until one solitary light is left. After the last point of sunlight has been blown out like a candle, the next stage of the total solar eclipse will begin.

The most dramatic stage has arrived! This is the third stage of the solar eclipse and is known as Totality. This is when the moon has totally covered the sun, allowing for no light to shine through. Not even a speck! You will notice that as the sky becomes darker, the temperature becomes colder. Even the birds stop chirping because they think that it is getting to be nighttime all of a sudden.

Now that the light of the sun has completely disappeared for a few minutes, don't panic because everything will soon be back to normal.

After the complete blackness of the Totality stage comes the next solar eclipse stage. This is the fourth stage and is called Third Contact. Since the moon has completely covered the sun during the Totality stage, it is now time to uncover it. You will be able to see the corona of the sun peeking out, giving the appearance of a diamond ring. The Baily's beads effect will occur once more as well. And that crescent sun shape looks so cool! Even the little mini crescents on the ground in the form of shadow bands will make another appearance!

The fifth and final stage of the solar eclipse is now ready to take effect. This is, you guessed it, the Fourth Contact stage. It's like playing the First Contact stage in reverse. The moon is now moving ever farther away from the sun. Then, the sun will soon appear as a circular sphere in the sky and the sky will look like its old self again on a bright and sunny day.

Did you know that there are other kinds of solar eclipses besides total solar eclipses? I know that total solar eclipses are the most exciting and the least frequently occurring, but that doesn't mean that other types of solar eclipses aren't worth viewing.

The annular solar eclipse, for example, allows the sun to cast a gold ring around the moon. In this instance, the moon is not large enough in appearance to completely cover the sun. The bright and shining ring around the moon is an impressive sight to see. My dad told me that the scientific word for this glowing ring effect is an annulus.

Then there's the partial solar eclipse. This is the most frequently occurring solar eclipse. Our Earth experiences a partial solar eclipse two times a year. In this type of solar eclipse, the path that the moon is travelling on cannot cover the sun completely, only partially. Much of the sun's surface remains visible. The sun appears in the shape of a thick crescent as the moon partially passes in front of it. A crescent sun! It's like watching a big cookie in the sky being eaten. Or like watching a crescent moon that is spinning around like the wheel of a moving car.

Lastly, the fourth type of solar eclipse is known as a hybrid solar eclipse. It is not quite a total eclipse, but it is also not quite an annular eclipse. A hybrid solar eclipse is something in between. Some people may see a total eclipse occurring, while others may see an annular eclipse. It all depends on your location.

My dad has already watched a total solar eclipse. This eclipse happened on August 21st of 2017, almost a year before I was born. It was the first time the United States had experienced a total eclipse since 1979. Of course, the year 1979 was five years before my dad was born. Imagine the sheer joy of watching a total solar eclipse for the first time. My dad wants me to experience the enthusiasm that he experienced when he watched the total solar eclipse from our own backyard. I am so excited that I invited my friends from school to watch the total solar eclipse with me in our family's backyard!

To be on the safe side, you must wear a special pair of sunglasses when watching a solar eclipse. These sunglasses are also known as "solar viewers." They look a lot like the glasses you wear when you're watching a movie in 3D. The lenses of these sunglasses are made of a synthetic material called polymer, which is ten—thousand times darker than regular sunglasses. Polymer helps to block out infrared and ultraviolet light, both of which can cause damage to your eyesight, leading to visual complications like cataracts or even blindness. As fun as it is to watch a solar eclipse, it is also very dangerous if it's not done safely. Always be sure that your solar viewers have been approved by the ISO. Then you know one hundred percent that your eyes will be fully protected from the brightness of the sun.

Now let's grab a bucket of popcorn and enjoy the upcoming 3D movie called Total Solar Eclipse playing for one time only on April 8th of 2024 in select cities across the United States, including mine! I hope you learned a lot about outer space and especially my dad's favorite activity, experiencing the solar eclipse.

Maybe the next time we meet, I will talk to you about lunar eclipses and how they work. Since my dad is an astrophysicist, he knows a lot about lunar eclipses too! There's actually a lunar eclipse coming up on March 25th of 2024, two weeks before the total solar eclipse event that we all have been waiting for! A lunar eclipse occurs when the moon orbits into the path of our Earth's shadow. Then, during the Totality stage of the lunar eclipse, the moon will go from bright and white to bright and red. The lunar eclipse will also occur past my bedtime, and I have school the next day. But maybe if I am good, my dad will let me watch some of it!

I am so excited to see my first total solar eclipse! I cannot wait to watch the solar eclipse and hope you will enjoy it too!